WISH UPON A GIGGLE!

D1716689

By Sue Hamilton Kloss

THIS BOOK BELONGS TO:

_____

For Stanley & Alex

May your world always be filled with magic

& may all your wishes in life come true!

OR A ROCKET SHIP THAT COULD FLY SO FAR?

IF YOU HAD A
MAGIC HORN,
WOULD YOU
WISH FOR A
PET UNICORN?

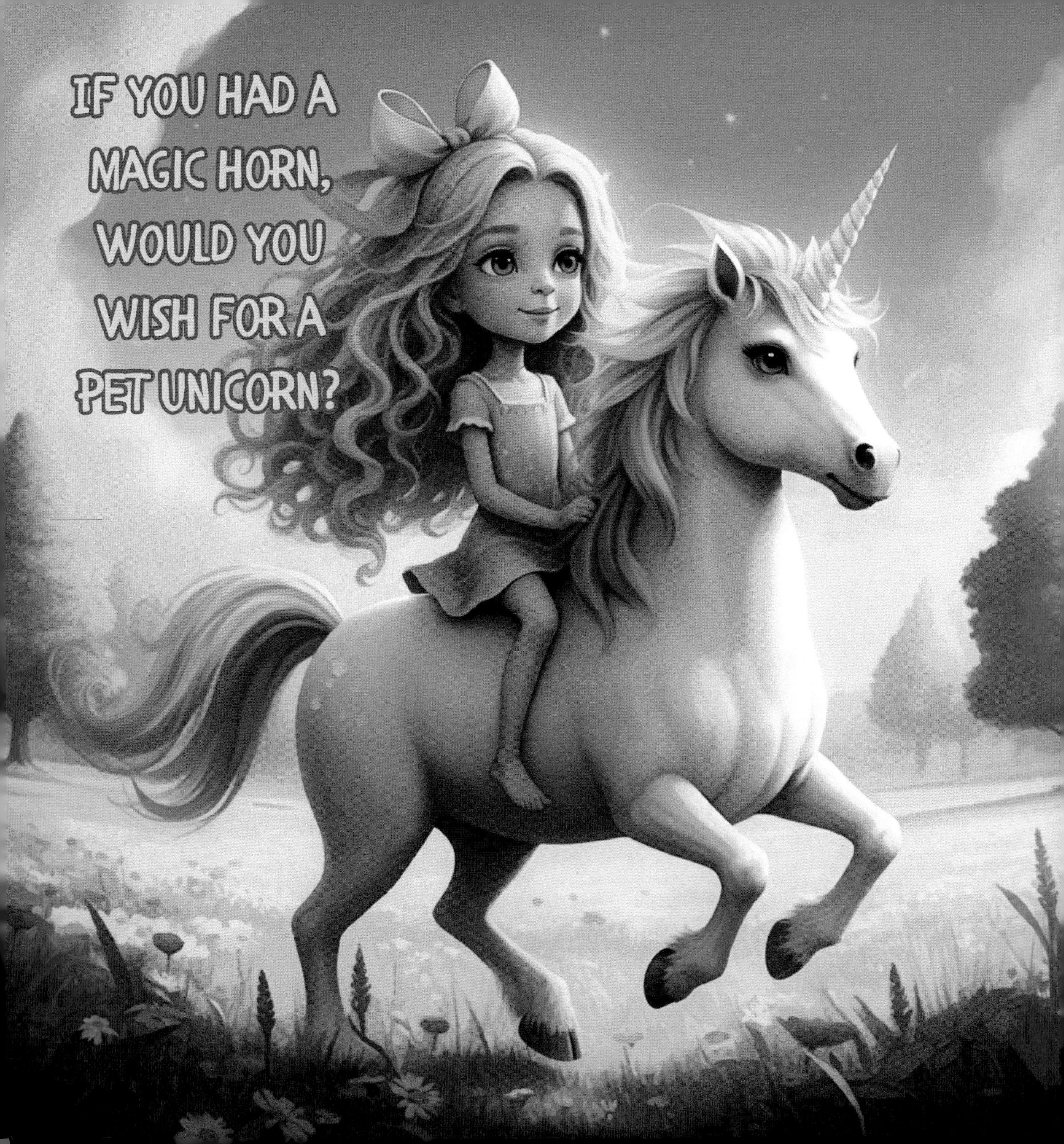

OR PERHAPS A CARNIVAL ON YOUR BACK LAWN?

OR HAVE GIANT WINGS SO YOU COULD FLY?

IF YOU HAD A MAGIC BUS,
WOULD YOU VISIT SOMEONE FAMOUS?

OR DRIVE SOMEWHERE MARVELOUS AND WONDEROUS?

IF YOU HAD A MAGIC DOOR, WOULD YOU LET IN A DINOSAUR?

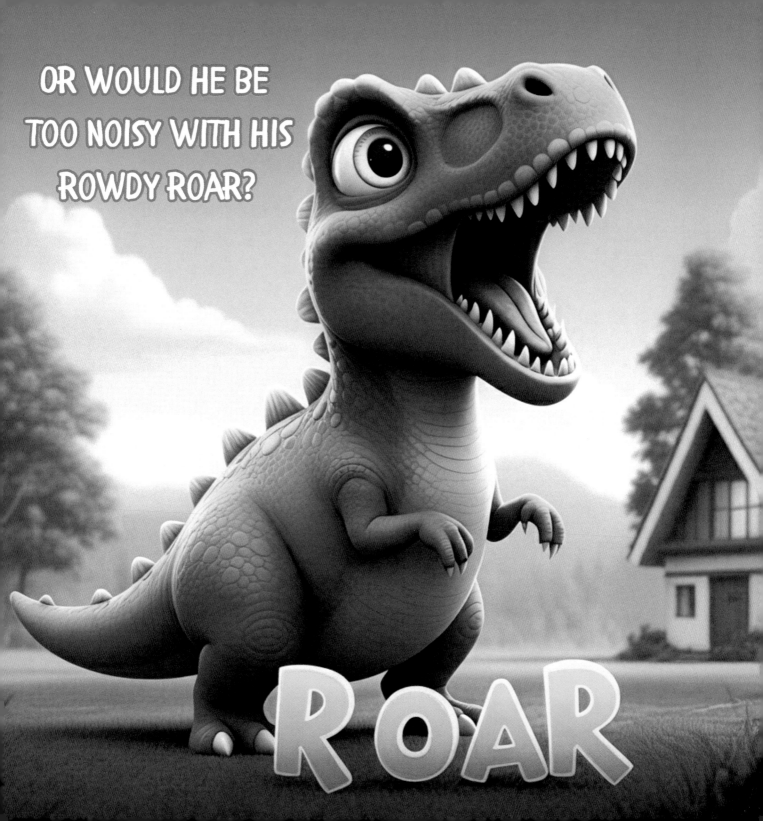

IF YOU HAD SOME MAGIC HONEY,
WOULD YOU SELL IT FOR A LOT OF MONEY?

OR WISH FOR A SNUGGLY CUDDLY BUNNY?

OR TO TURN THE CLASS BULLY INTO A MULE?

IF YOU HAD A MAGIC MOTHER, WOULD YOU WISH FOR ANOTHER SISTER OR BROTHER?

IF YOU HAD A MAGIC SHEEP, WOULD YOU WISH TO NEVER FALL ASLEEP?

OR WOULD A SHEEP BE TOO HARD TO KEEP?

ONE LAST WISH,
IS GRANTED FOR YOU,
READ THESE WORDS
AND IT MAY COME TRUE!

I WISH I MAY,
I WISH I MIGHT,
BE GRANTED THE WISH,
I WISH TONIGHT!

About the Author......

Sue is a bit of a gypsy who has lived in 5 different countries and 28 houses all around the world. Sue is married, has two BIG kids and lives in Virginia, USA.....for now!

Her great loves are her family, travelling and creating joy through her books.

She also has a deep passion for laughter because......

laughter is the universal language of happiness!

63745809R00018

Made in the USA
Middletown, DE
05 November 2024